The Sky's the Limit

TONY CHRISTIANSEN
talks to Angie Belcher

Learning Media

Contents

It was a beautiful Friday. Tony Christiansen
and his friends were playing in the school
grounds. They swung on the junglegym and
kicked a ball to each other. They ran around
the field playing tag. Tony had no idea that this
was the last time he would ever do these things.

The only photo of me with legs

> **"It's not what happens
> to you that counts . . .
> it's what you do about it."**

I can still remember the accident, just like it was yesterday.

It was a Saturday morning. My friend Gary came by. "Let's go over to the rail yards and help to bag some coal," he said. This was one of the ways our neighborhood club raised money. That sounded great to me, so we ran down to the yards together. We were crossing the tracks behind some rail wagons when the wagons suddenly rolled backwards. Nobody really knows why. It was just one of those things. I got knocked over, and the wheels ran over my legs. I was nine years old.

5

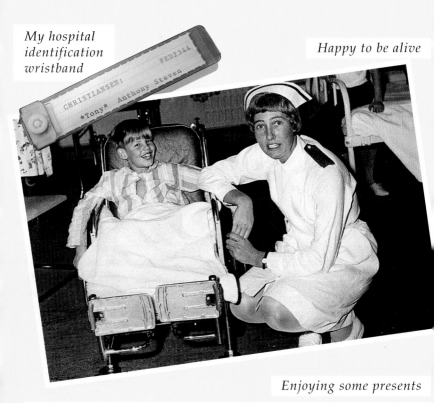

My hospital identification wristband

CHRISTIANSEN: FED2344
Tony Anthony Steven

Happy to be alive

Enjoying some presents

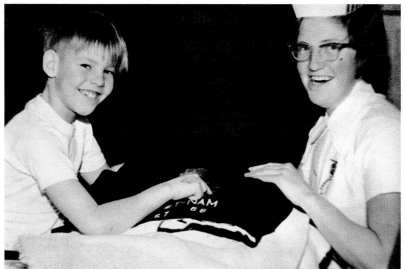

I was in hospital for seven months. I had to learn how to move all over again – with no legs to help me this time. At first, all I could do was roll about. As I got stronger, I learned how to sit up straight. Then I could move around on my bottom and hands. I was on the move again. Nothing was going to stop me!

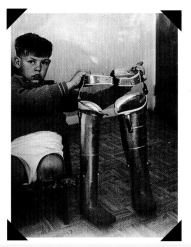

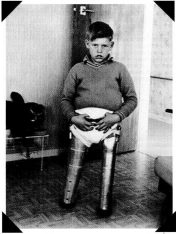

My first legs, called "rockers"

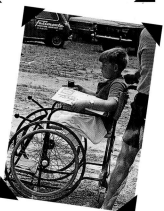

Sink or swim

*M*om and Dad had some friends who were swimming coaches. They told us that swimming was great exercise. It would help me a lot. But I hated water. I didn't swim before my accident, and now I didn't have any legs. "How can this work?" I wondered. Well, it was simple. Mom and Dad sat me on the edge of the pool. Then they pushed me into the water. If I didn't swim, I was going to sink to the bottom of the pool.

I sank. As I was going under for the third time, they grabbed a big net. It was the kind you use to get the leaves out of the pool. They used it to scoop me out of the water. I thought that was the end of learning to swim. But everyone wanted me to try again, and again. So, at first, we set small goals. Then bigger ones.

Five months after that first day, exactly one year after the accident, I swam fifty-two lengths of the pool. That's a whole mile – non-stop! Now I knew I could do whatever I wanted if I had "the right attitude."

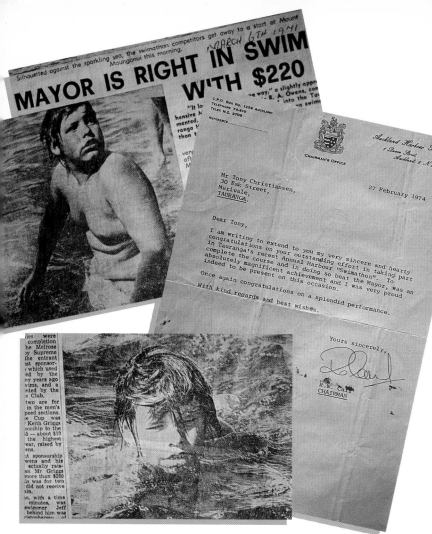

Silhouetted against the sparkling sea, the swimathon competitors get away to a start at Mount Maunganui this morning.

MARCH 6TH 1971

MAYOR IS RIGHT IN SWIM
WITH $220

les were
completion
he Melrose
by Supreme
the entrant
est sponsor-
which used
ed by the
ny years ago
vims, and i
nted by the
s Club.
two are for
in the men's
peed sections.
ie Cup was
Keith Griggs
sorship to the
5 — about $10
the highest
ear, raised by
ens.
it sponsorship
wens and his
actually rais-
an Mr Griggs
more than $260
is was for two
did not receive
in.
ie, with a time
minutes, was
swimmer Jeff
behind him was
ristopherson of

CHAIRMAN'S OFFICE

Auckland Harbour
1 Queen Street
Auckland 1, N.

Mr Tony Christiansen,
30 Esk Street,
Merivale,
TAURANGA.

27 February 1974

Dear Tony,

I am writing to extend to you my very sincere and hearty congratulations on your outstanding effort in taking part in Tauranga's recent Annual Harbour "Swimathon". To complete the course and in doing so beat the Mayor, was an absolutely magnificent achievement and I was very proud indeed to be present on this occasion.

Once again congratulations on a splendid performance.

With kind regards and best wishes.

Yours sincerely,

R.W. Ca
CHAIRMAN

When I got to high school, there were all kinds of sports and activities to choose from. I couldn't play football or soccer, but I could swim really well.

So I went to a surf lifesaving camp. At the end of the week, I had my bronze surf medal. After that I joined the local surf club. I wanted to start to help some of the

people in the community who had helped me.

THE SURF LIFE SAVING ASSOCIATION OF NEW ZEALAND

Surf Bronze Medallion

THIS IS TO CERTIFY that A. S. CHRISTIANSEN

a member of the Omanu Pacific Surf Life Saving Club

has qualified for the above award.

Hon. Registrar

Dated this 22nd day of Feb 19 76

Award No. 10911

VIGILANCE · SERVICE · ENDURANCE

I took part in thirty-three rescues at the surf club. There's one that I'll never forget. Three teenagers were caught out in the surf. I swam to one young girl while my buddy went after the other two. I put the rescue tube around her and told her everything was OK. Then we swam for the beach. When we got to the shallow water, I told her to walk. She stood up, took one look at me, with the water still up to my neck, … and fainted!

Amputee meets life's challenges head on

By Catherine Walton

It was Tony Christiansen's turn to do the rescue when a young boy in a plastic boat drifted out past the breakers at Omanu beach.

He grabbed a tube, swam out to the frightened boy, then helped him back through the surf.

"He was walking in waist-deep water when I was looked at me. The water was still up to my neck," Tony Christiansen said.

It was easy when they got that up to the water that he shakes his legs.

Steering with a group of sweaters at a Rotorua buttercup this week, the teenage figure-flier was happy to admit his life since he lost both legs in an accident 25 years ago.

Amputated

He hopes his own easy adjustment will help other people in a similar position.

The legs were amputated just below his torso after he was run over by a train when he was

He wore artificial legs for a while, but they kept falling off, so there then away and worked out his own way of doing things.

He relies on his wheelchair, but has also developed a massive strength in his upper torso and arms to compensate for the missing legs.

Something as simple as a swim involves all sorts of difficulties whatever his chair out.

Tony Christiansen wheeled his chair up and the sand at the Takipu Motorcamp pool before, then pulled himself off the chair onto the ground and hoped along the jetty into the water.

When he pushed off all the jetty into the water, his disability was hidden for a while as he swam around like anyone else, but you realised again how many adjustments he had to make when he come out.

You know how hard it is to pull yourself out of the water onto a jetty or boat? Try doing it with no legs.

His main love is swimming. You can't understand how some people can't swim, the thinks it's the easiest thing in the world.

Technique

But what about the technique? Without legs to float, wouldn't your lower leg just sink? Tony Christiansen isn't really interested in the explanation.

"I don't think about it — I just do it. I just love swimming and mucking around in water. Ironically he couldn't swim before his accident. He's conquered the water since, sitting on the edge of the pool, watching others swim.

After his morning swim, Tony showered along and wheeled out to his car, into which he took him about a minute to transfer from the instructor had taken over again. Watching you work they put it in the car.

But he soon realised that it was just the water is a novelty.

Lifesaver

Now he's a registered lifesaver at Omanu Surf Club.

But he's got anything a go.

He can do midget racers and off-readers which he used to take part in just

The younger boy, aged 8, must have gone to school and boasted about his father, says Tony Christiansen.

"Last year, when I went to the school gala day he was standing up all his friends to come and look at me and going. "See!"

Tony Christiansen is

Success for amputee

Legless lifesaver: HE'S GOT GUTS!

This amputee's a real flier

HANDICAPPED is just a word to 20-year-old Tony Christiansen

We haven't had any urge to speak of since he had an accident

Ever, despite this, the personable young Tauranga apprentice has parked more physical achievement onto his short life than most able-bodied people manage in a lifetime.

An associated visitors to beautiful Omanu Beach see the legless lifesaver plummeting across the surf sand

Enthusiasm

With his enthusiasm for life Tony Christiansen started competing in Air NorGus few are

spinaky youck is not only that local surf club's chosen team captain but also the holder of an incredible eight gold medals in international competitions.

"He was dead keen," says Mr Tony Christiansen and this

Award surprise lifesave

Nov 3- 1978.

TAURANGA double leg amputee Mr Tony Christiansen has received a high award from the Lifesaving world.

certainly had no idea it was to receive an award like this.

Enjoyed

Tony first became interested in surf lifesaving after taking it as an option at school, something I

but at the moment I'll see how things go. Bay of Plenty Surf Lifesaving Association's lifesaving Officer, Mr Frankha

Then we enc
could feel
opportunity
of lifesa
The Mr

Looking like everyone else

I missed a lot of school after the accident. I missed even more while I was fitted with artificial legs. I had to wear them to school so I would look like all the other kids. But it was hard work walking around because each leg weighed nearly twenty pounds.

Upright ... and standing tall

13

A lot of people helped me at school, but one of the school's football coaches became a special friend. He had no legs either. One day he tried to kick the ball over the goal post. His artificial leg went flying through the air instead of the ball. I've never seen anything so funny. That one little thing made me realize that it doesn't matter what you look like. It's how you think and your sense of humor that matter most of all.

The best family I could have

Walking around on those legs made me very tired, so at lunchtime I sometimes rested while my friends played outside. That was when I started to draw. Cartoons and letters were my favorites. After a while, I started to get good at it. I found that I could make money out of the lettering. While my friends delivered papers after school, I did sign writing for stores. I made five times as much money as my friends did!

When I left school, I decided that I wanted to be a sign writer. At first, no one would give me a job. "You can't climb ladders. You can't drive a truck," they all said. I knew I *could*

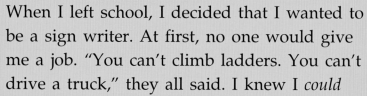

do all of those things if they gave me the chance. I didn't give up, though. A few years later, I had my own sign writing business with seven other people working for me!

My ladders of success

I didn't like artificial legs. When I stood up, they never pointed the right way. It was much easier to be in my wheelchair or to shuffle around on my bottom. I didn't mind not looking like everyone else. I wanted to be myself.

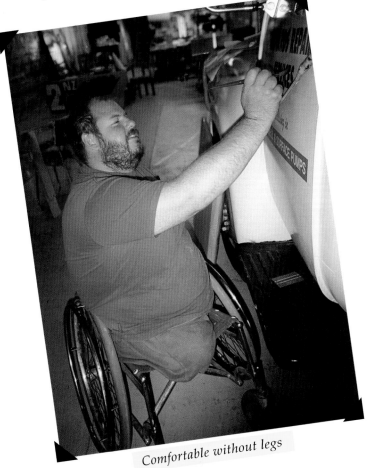

Comfortable without legs

There's no such word as "can't"

$\mathcal{H}$aving no legs didn't stop me from being like my brother and sister. I climbed trees.

"Grab the rope and tow me again"

I rode my sister's horse and my brother's bike. We lived near a steep hill. I used to sit on the bike, and when I was ready, the other kids would let me go. I loved the freedom and the speed.

The need for speed

From this ...

My father built me a **go-kart**, and soon I was leaving the other kids in the dust. Racing was in my blood.

... to this

... TO THIS!

... *Tony's di*

12 BAY OF PLENTY TIMES, FRIDAY, NOVEMBER 22, 1996

Horsepower puts a smile on Tony's di

By Colin Smith

THERE'S been an ear to ear grin on Tony Christiansen's face this week. It's been a permanent fixture since the Tauranga racer made his sprint car debut at Western Springs last Saturday night.

"I'm still fizzing," says the former midget car racer about his return to the Speedway ranks — a move which fulfills a long held ambition to campaign a sprint car.

And from the first time the double amputee racer twisted his hand operated throttle on 650 horsepower, he was hooked.

"It's awesome. It really gives you a kick in the pants when you get on the throttle.

"Corner to corner the sprint car is so much quicker than a midget."

The sprint car venture with a 410 cubic inch Chevrolet powered Gambler chassis is the latest phase in Christiansen's motorsports career which has also included karting, offroad racing and most recently a move into Pre-65 saloon car racing with a Mark 3 Ford Zephyr.

"I've enjoyed circuit racing but I really felt back at home again on the dirt . . . have gone back

done" Saturday night first taste convinced he'd made the right decision.

"It was everything I expected and more," he says.

"It was good because I was able to learn things about what I was doing and we

TONY CHRISTIANSE

TONY Christiansen has joined the sprint car ranks at Western Springs.   Photo: Colin Smith

Bay of Plenty Speedway
Assoc. Inc.

Certificate

Trip Away Travel   Trophy

Presented to   Tony Christiansen   6m

For Highest points Feature for Midgets

Season   1991-92

R.P.Duncan
President

A.Campbell.
Secretary

I look like R2D2 from "Star Wars"

I always enjoy winning!

When I got older,
I started racing cars – sprint cars,
saloon cars, and midgets. I called all of my
cars "Toenails." When you sit in a car and put
a helmet on, you're just like everyone else.

I've had my share of accidents too. Once I was in a car rally. I had no legs, and my driver had one artificial leg. We came to a bad corner, and the car rolled over into some sand. We weren't hurt, but my driver's artificial leg came off. As we crawled out of the car, someone saw us and called for an ambulance. "There's been a terrible accident," they said. "One guy has lost his leg, and the other guy is buried up to his waist in the sand!" When we heard that, we just couldn't stop laughing.

I love motorcycles too. Trail riding is fun, but sometimes I have trouble staying on the seat. My friends say I should put Velcro on my pants, or maybe stick to riding in the sidecar!

Nothing scares me

Sometimes I would hear people saying "I can't do that." That made me want to go out there and prove that if I could do it with no legs, then they could do it with two. If you go through life thinking you *can't*, then you won't. My parents always said to me, "You can do anything you want to do - you just have to get out there and try!"

23

One step at a time

After the accident, I learned to set goals – that means thinking about something you really want to do. Then you work out the best way to do it – one step at a time.

Life to me is a rac

When I was fifteen years old, I was watching the Olympic Games on TV. "Wouldn't it be awesome to be in something like the Olympics?" I thought. So I set myself a goal and worked out how to get there. I started learning how to throw the shot put, the discus, and the javelin, and I took part in track events.

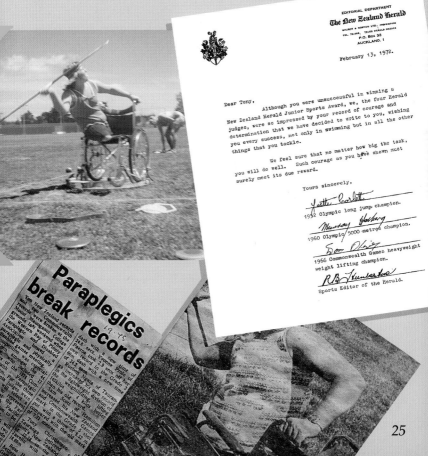

Paraplegics break records

25

I really wanted to get to the World Games, and to win. Since then, I've been to the World Games six times, and I have thirty-five medals – twelve gold, seventeen silver, and six bronze.

The first of many medals

Recognition at last

A proud moment with the t

I know that as long as my goals aren't really impossible, I can do almost anything. So, it's no good wanting to play soccer in the World Cup – that just isn't going to happen. But there are lots of other things that I can do.

L AND MOBILE ON COURT

MR CHRISTIANSEN dives to play a shot

abled athlete tries squash

No time to stop … life's too short … like me!

When I started going to tae kwon do, everyone thought I was crazy.

"How can you learn tae kwon do?" they said. "It's like karate. You have to use your arms and legs to do the moves."

But tae kwon do isn't just self-defense. It's a way of thinking and living. My instructor showed me how to use a walking stick to help with some of the moves.

I was so proud when I received my belts – white, yellow, green, blue, and red. Then the ultimate goal – my Black Belt and 2nd Degree Black Belt.

제N-96 호 **단 증**
초 단

주소: 73. JAMES COOK DRIVE TAURANGA
성명: 토니 크리스챤스
생년월일: 서기1958년 10월23일생

상기자는 제42회 승단심사
결과 본회 규정에 의하여 자
격을 수여함
서기 1989년 5월20일

뉴질랜드 태킨도 협회

회장 이 정 남

CERTIF

NAME TONY CHRISTIA
ADDRESS 73 JAMES COOK
DATE OF BIRTH 23 OCT 1958
BLACK BELT / ST

THIS IS TO CERTIFY THAT T
NAMED ABOVE HAS ATTAIN
DAN IN THE 42ND TAE KW
PROMOTION TEST CONDUCTED
NEW ZEALAND TAE-KWON L
FEDERATION

Jung Nam Lee
PRESIDENT
N.Z.T.K.D. FEDERATION

Black belt with whee

The sky's the limit

I guess you could say that when I set a goal, I "reach for the sky." So nobody was surprised when I said I wanted to learn how to fly. I'd been up in gliders. I'd done a tandem parachute jump. I knew there had to be some way that I could fly a plane. I have a friend who is a flying instructor. He asked other instructors all around the world for help. We found out that there *was* a way to do it. There are other pilots who can't use their legs. They use a kind of hand control to fly the plane instead. I knew that if I could find one of these hand controls, then I could learn to fly.

My dream of flight

Before long, I had the special control and a very helpful teacher. For me, one of the hardest parts of learning to fly was getting in and out of the plane.

Flying solo for the first time was a real buzz!

Bay of Plenty Flight Centre

Flight Training Specialists

CERTIFICATE OF SOLO

THIS IS TO ACKNOWLEDGE
ON TUESDAY 24TH MARCH 1998

TONY CHRISTIANSEN

FLEW ALONE AND UNASSISTED
A CESSNA 172
TAKE OFF FROM AND SAFELY RETURNED TO
TAURANGA AIRPORT

Thereby completing a "First Solo Flight" and joining the elite group of persons who have successfully defied the law of gravity and qualified for this recognition

Signed _____

Phil Hooker
Chief Flying Instructor

Sometimes people think that because I don't have legs, I don't have a brain or feelings either. That's been a hard thing to deal with. Some people don't understand that everyone has dreams and that disabled people are just like them.

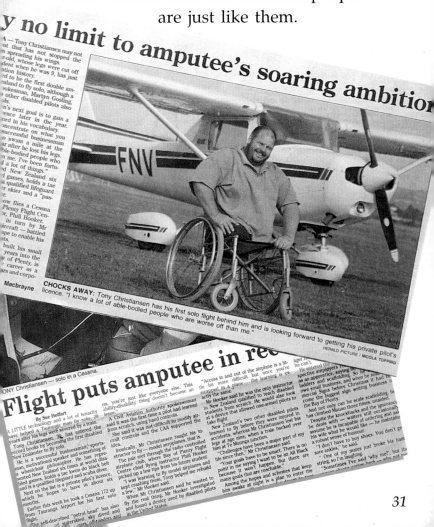

y no limit to amputee's soaring ambition

CHOCKS AWAY: Tony Christiansen has his first solo flight behind him and is looking forward to getting his private pilot's licence. "I know a lot of able-bodied people who are worse off than me."

HERALD PICTURE / NICOLA TOPPING

Flight puts amputee in re...

Tony Christiansen is married and has three grown-up children. Tony travels around the world speaking to groups of people and teaching them how important it is to follow their dreams. Tony's next goal is to learn to ski and then take part in the Winter Olympics.

Life doesn't get any better than this!